WHOLENESS IN ILLNESS

WHOLENESS IN ILLNESS

Roberta S. Poorman, D. Min.
with
John P. Poorman

Sheepstone Farm Press
Schoharie NY 12157

First edition, January 2014 (r2.02.17.14)

ISBN 978-1-304-78745-3

ACKNOWLEDGEMENTS:

Biblical references are from the New International Version (NIV), International Bible Society, except where noted.

Poem "*Whale's Lament*" by John P. Poorman.

Additional copies for purchase at www.lulu.com

CONTENTS

Introduction 1

Chapter 1: Fearfully and Wonderfully Made.......... 5

Chapter 2: A Question of Identity.......................... 9

Chapter 3: A Theology of Suffering 23

Chapter 4: The Journey 35

Chapter 5: Comforting along the Way 73

The Whale's Lament

The sharks swim swiftly in the blue, blue, blue ocean. The whales fly low and speak softly to the waves. The fish are not whales, and the whales know that they are not fish. They squeal, "How high must I fly to reach beyond the water, to seek the air which has no bounds? The water is heavy and dark and wet. And I am heavy and dark and wet. Why must there be whales? Why must there be sharks? Why can't we fly high?

"I love to fly. I like to swim. But swim is all that I can do, and I am not allowed to feel the air or caress the breeze. Soft, soft, soft is the air. Wet, deep, harsh is the sea. Life began here, but moved on. Why cannot I? Must I stay? Must I sink? I know more than this, but life confines; it limits; it stifles creativity. I need not be a whale. I can fly, and I know I can. Oh gravity! Oh water! Oh weight! Why is the world so big and I so big and life so small?

"Slice, spin, swirl, dive. Emerge from the sea. Challenge the law, make life anew! God is in his place, I am in mine, and I am his. My place is here, and I am known in the ebony recesses which struggle for light. I am heard above the soft chatter of the surface and my sound is sweet. I will not rebel. I am not alone and I am at peace, if not with my lot then with my calling. And I shall not complain again for I am the master of my place."

INTRODUCTION

A Lifelong Journey

Millions of people in the United States live with chronic, painful, "invisible", debilitating conditions such as lupus, chronic fatigue immune deficiency syndrome (CFIDS) and fibromyalgia. And many, many more who are struggling yet are misdiagnosed or undiagnosed. Ours is a very lonely life. Our illnesses are invisible. Our symptoms are confusing, even to us.

Add to these the sizeable numbers of individuals grappling with more visible conditions such as multiple sclerosis, cancer, neuromuscular and other diseases and the need for understanding is multiplied several-fold.

This book is not a guide to miraculous recovery, although we will be exploring the miraculous.

This book is not the dramatic story of my illness, though I will share my experiences with you.

This book is not a Bible study, though we will study the Bible as it relates to our experiences with these chronic illnesses.

This book is a suggestion of some new ways of looking at our illnesses.

This book is about journey.

This journey is one of hope.

This is your book. I hope that you will find yourself someplace in these pages.

This is a book for your family and friends; for those who want to share your journey.

This is not to be rushed. I suggest that you try not to skim through the material, but rather to move slowly, pondering some of the ideas, allowing pieces of it to resonate with your own experience.

We will also cover much of the ground more than once. Sometimes our limited capacity for learning difficult concepts requires coming at the same material from various angles. Don't get impatient. Read, ponder and own for yourself whatever stories or phrases are helpful to you.

My journey took a major turn decades years ago when I was diagnosed with lupus, then later with fibromyalgia and eventually with serious complications from rheumatoid and osteoarthritis and renal failure. For over ten years during my work at New Horizons Christian Counseling Center, a large portion of my clients presented with issues around lupus, fibromyalgia, CFIDS and other chronic conditions. I have been privileged to walk alongside them as they contemplated wholeness in the face of illness. And now you and I have the opportunity to walk this trail together.

Accept the fact that no one else can fully understand what you are going through. Don't expect the experiences I describe to match yours completely. Our journeys must be different from each other, even if we share the same conditions.

Finally, as a Christian pastoral counselor, the belief system I use includes the following concepts which will be discussed as they arise:

1. *We are part of God's creation.*
2. *We are created in the image of God.*
3. *God's creation is fallen.*
4. *God offers comfort, hope, redemption.*
5. *God uses our condition for ministry.*

Shall we begin?

1

FEARFULLY AND WONDERFULLY MADE

A Word about Our Foundation

One of the most important things I can do for my clients is to remind them that they were an idea in the mind of God before their parents ever contemplated their conception. I remind them that God tells us it is our existence which makes His creation not just good but very good, not just pleasing to God but very pleasing. I try to help them understand that their one solitary life is important. God is the "Omni-God"; He is the all-knowing, all-powerful, the all-present God. But He is also the personal God who lives within us:

> *"For you created my inmost being;*
>
> *You knit me together in my mother's womb.*
>
> *I praise you because I am fearfully and wonderfully made;*
>
> *Your works are wonderful,*
>
> *I know that full well."* (Psalm 139:13-14)

He is the God who knows my thoughts before I do:

> *"O Lord, You have searched me and you know me.*
>
> *You know when I sit and when I rise;*
>
> *You perceive my thoughts from afar.*
>
> *You discern my going out and my lying down;*
>
> *You are familiar with all my ways.*
>
> *Before a word is on my tongue you know it completely, O Lord."*
>
> (Psalm 139: 1-4)

Who I am and what I am about is no accident. We are intentional.

But who am I, *really*? Some of the most common questions heard in therapy sessions revolve around personal identity To answer this question we need to begin with Genesis where we are told that we are part of the created universe, made from the very soil on which we walk. Even the word "adam" arises from the Hebrew word for dirt or earth. This suggests we are connected with all creation and with its movement we resonate. Yet we are not mere creatures. We are not merely the victims of cause and effect. We have been created in God's image. That means many things.

For example, we are imbued with the capacity for reason, and for power and authority. We think and we try to solve problems. Our thoughts and actions carry powerful consequences. Being made in the image of God means we have a sense of right and wrong, fair and unfair. Regardless of how closely our value system reflects God's (or differs from it), as human beings we are compelled to be conscious of right and wrong in a way that the rest of creation was not made to experience.

Being made in God's image also means that we pursue goals and feel an inherent need for purpose in our lives. We share the verb "create" with no other creature than God. (The beaver building his dam and the bird feathering her nest are just replicating, not creating. A bird's nest is very different indeed from a painting, a symphony or the design of an airplane.)

Finally, recognizing the image of God within us explains the need to be in relationship not only with other living things but also with God – after all, we are by nature spiritual beings. And we carry a cognizance of God's existence that none of our animal brethren share.

The attributes which we share with God are indeed what makes us human but they are also the characteristics on which our own individual, personal identity is formed and frequently challenged. As we grow and mature and experience life, much of the question,

"Who am I?" will be asked and answered in direct relationship to the attributes which we share with God and in the context of our relationship with God. "What is my purpose? Where do I fit in the overall scheme of things? Is life fair?"

Within the Judeo-Christian tradition we find celebration of the individual and the community in both ideal splendor and chaotic dysfunction. The Bible provides the framework by which we can clarify the context, purpose and process of human experience. In Genesis as throughout Scripture, we are given the opportunity to watch humanity as it plummets from its lofty perfection almost to its tragic demise. The story of Adam, of Abraham, of all the very flawed heroes of the Bible provides a narrative with which we can all identify, within which we can find a way to understand life as we know it. This is our foundation.

2

A QUESTION OF IDENTITY

We are created as part of creation and have a unique place in it .We are very susceptible to elements within creation that would destroy us. Yet, at the same time, we are so powerful that we hold the power to destroy one another or the whole planet. But we can only be successful when we understand the problems, explore the solutions and take control of our resources. Our ability to do this depends on our perception and interpretation of all that we experience.

This experience begins early. Until the day we die we will be learning, unlearning and relearning lessons from life. What we learn has much to do with how we frame our experiences in terms of our identity.

From Mind of God to Womb

While the call to live out God's image is God-given, this begs another question. Why do I specifically deal with my reality the way I do? Where do my value systems originate? Why do some things "push my buttons" but not affect someone else? Where do I find my sense of self-worth?

Part of the answer is revealed through careful observation. It seems that we are all molded to see the world and ourselves in certain ways. Ways that differ from person to person. We're molded by experience.

Thanks to Margaret Mahler, Louise Kaplan and others who have dedicated their careers to helping us gain understanding of the developing human mind, we are able as adults to get a sense of how we each came to our personal world view.[1] We know that while still in the utopian environment of the womb, our perception and cognition skills are already being awakened. The "almost baby" is exposed to sound and touch and temperature and total immediate gratification. That is of course, assuming that this is a normal pregnancy. When physical abuse occurs to the mother, loud angry voices penetrate the uterine wall. When toxic drugs or anxiety-laden hormones flow from the mother to the unborn child, we know our little person is already being traumatized and these traumas will affect what he or she expects from life and how he will understand the things to come.

When Anita was still a fetus, her mother had been in a physically and verbally abusive relationship with her father. Though the mother had divorced her father soon after Anita was born, the abuse had affected her. While still in that usually all-gratifying world of the uterus, Anita had heard the sounds and felt the blows of trauma. Later, when Anita was two and half years old, her mother was in a car accident and hospitalized for six months. During that time Anita was cared for by a series of baby sitters. To complicate matters further, Anita had been a very colicky baby. With all these early experiences of pain and separation from mother, it was not a surprise when her basic response to the pain and fatigue of CFIDS was one of despair. She had learned from experience that comforting and soothing could not be counted on. It would be hard for her to seek out help and to develop the positive mental attitude she would need to help herself.

For those of us whose utopian experience of the womb is uninterrupted, trauma still awaits us at birth. In the worst possible scenario, our wet, warm, soft world of muffled, soothing sounds is suddenly obliterated by piercing lights, hard cold metal and loud strange voices -- then someone slaps as. Even with the newer water birthing techniques it is clear right away that utopia is a thing of the past. But its memory, in primitive symbolic form, stays with us.

---

[1] See Mahler, M. S., Pine, F., and Bergman, A., *The Psychological Birth of the Human Infant,* Basic Books, New York, NY, 1978. Also, Kaplan, Louise J., PhD., *Oneness and Separateness,* Simon and Schuster, New York, NY, 1998.

We have no words or logic with which to frame it or communicate it, but it remains just the same.

From Womb to Imperfect World

God, who always prepares the way, is gracious and provides us with sensory barriers so that we are not too discomforted too quickly. Our little eyes and ears are quite limited in what they can do. Our little brain is gathering its first pieces of reality. We do not quite understand that Mom and I are not still one unit. We still feel symbiotically tied together. Gratification is not so immediate and definitely not so reliable. And what if the birth is difficult or there are complications and mother and infant are separated? This is the first primal experience of abandonment. But even without a crisis the baby learns that there is coming and going and that he must take some initiative. So he cries and finds appendages that might gratify his hunger, a fist here, a foot there and then that other thing that he believes to be as much a part of him and as much under his control as the others but this one is different.

Eventually as he matures, he figures out that the gratifier is indeed separate from him and also unreliable, so much so that there are seemingly two mommies -- the "good mommy" who fulfills and the "bad mommy" who withholds. If every baby in this fallen world experiences the disappointment of imperfect mommies, imagine the effect of a mentally or physically ill, over-stressed, or emotionally unavailable mom. What happens when caregivers change unpredictably and holding and cooing and smiles aren't sufficiently reliable?

From years of intensive research we know that the child's inner sense of security and lovability is threatened. He is already learning that life hurts and that there are no saviors. Depending on the intensity of the felt abandonment and the core personality of the child, he will begin to develop alternative resources that work for now but could easily become dysfunctional at later stages of life.

Alternatively, if the mom fails to allow the child to experience disappointment through exposure to the bad disappointing mommy, then that child's view of self and world is again distorted and the little person will have troubled tolerating and integrating frustration later on. Mom just needs to manage to gratify enough while imparting other values as the baby grows.[2] This means that the baby has the consistent, attuned, warm, safe, and empathic and responsible maternal environment he needs to continue his exploration.

It won't take him long to figure out that life is complex and that "Good Mom" and "Bad Mom" are the same person. It won't take much longer for him to discover the world of manipulation. Daily and weekly his world will grow. His awareness of his own powers will increase. He will begin to travel (with his face to the floor of course). Then that moment will come when he is upright, standing tall, hands free and available for real research. He finds he can entertain and he can frustrate.

I remember a very special moment, when I was directing the Family Ministry program at City Mission in Schenectady NY. We had finished our evening with the ladies and children in the parenting program. The ladies were sitting in a circle and we were singing. I remember we were singing "Father Abraham". The children were in the middle of the circle and they were singing and doing the movements. They were stamping their feet and they were singing. There was one little boy named Eric. He had blond hair and blue eyes and rosy cheeks. And as we sang and in his little one-and-a-half-year-old way, he too was clapping his hands and singing with all his energy. And then the magic moment happened. All of a sudden, Eric looked around and he saw all the faces in the circle and they were all smiling at him. And Eric felt special. He felt powerful. And he stamped his feet, he clapped his hands, and he sang with all his strength. He would never have a moment like that again. He was so powerful. He could make people smile. And as that moment, he feels almost like he is God.

---

[2] See works by Winnicott, D. W. on the concept of ego psychology. Winnicott is credited for coining the term "good enough mother" to describe the ideal parent.

This is a special time for Eric. It is the opening up of a New World. He can even talk and share his innermost thoughts. From now on things will never be the same, because now he knows that he is a person.

These months are precious to all parents but in the busyness of life, parents often fail to recognize that this is the most intense period of emotional as well as physical development. Ages one through three determine who this child is; the core personality is molded into a person through these early experiences of self and world, of me and "not me". And this molding comes as reality is filtered through the mother (or primary caregiver) to the child. From conception until kindergarten mother is the world. Her health, her moods, her personality, her values color how the child understands self and all that is not self.

Why this long discourse? Because our experience with illness and suffering is going to be powerfully affected by what we internalize through Mom as infants and toddlers. Is it okay to be dependent? Can doctors be trusted? Why me? Is it safe to look for comfort from anyone? Is God (as the heavenly father or mother) someone to help me or cast me aside because I have little worth? These questions and their various answers arise in large measure from this period.

These questions and their answers also arise from the larger family environment. As we are exposed to fathers and siblings and aunts and uncles and grandparents, they will frustrate and excite us because they are different from Mom. We will be challenged and we will constantly practice being people. And we will continue to be molded. That's what families do. Families build societies not vice versa.

Self and Family

As we read through Genesis we follow the story of the family. The first man and woman were also the first parents and they were told to have children, not just to populate the earth but to pass on and recreate the image of God. (Genesis 1:27-28) Of course, we all realize that what gets passed down from generation to generation is closer to the image of Adam than the image of God. Lying, scheming, cheating, hating, killing are passed along by the same individuals that defend the name of Yahweh.

Families continue to do the same today. They pass on their values and beliefs and traditions. Family values, beliefs and traditions that are, at best, informed by Scripture, but in any case, imperfect because of the reality of a fallen world.

When Martha first walked into my office, I couldn't help but notice how controlled she was. She stood tall and straight. She moved gracefully. Even as she sat in the easy chair I offered her, there was a stiffness about her for her hands were clasped in her lap and her ankles were politely crossed. Her statements were polite and appropriate, yet, as she responded to my questions what she was telling did not fit with her body language. Six months earlier she had been diagnosed with fibromyalgia. She was in my office now, she said, because she was having trouble coping. She described her symptoms and the impact on life and yet her tone of voice was detached as if she was giving me the weather report. After listening for a while, I interrupted her and asked her how she was feeling now, in my office at this moment. She finally began to describe feelings rather than terminology and began to exhibit the body language of someone experiencing fibromyalgia. Now her suffering is in the room and we could begin to address it.

Why had there been such contradictions between what Martha felt and the way she expressed yourself? I asked her that. She had no idea. Then I asked questions about her family and things began to make sense. Both of her parents were teachers, her dad in math and her mother in bio-chemistry. Her mother had a Ph.D. Her father had partially finished his Master's degree program. There was a strong sense of pride in intellectual accomplishments in her family. There was also a family heritage on her mother's side of a certain degree of social status that was no longer accompanied by finances. Martha was the oldest of five children all born within a year two of one another. And Martha related that her mother has regrets for the years spent in child-rearing. Her mother had stayed home until the youngest child was in kindergarten and then she'd returned to teaching.

With this information I began to make some assumptions about Martha's belief system. It was just possible that Martha had never been taught that it is okay to be sick. Martha described herself as a "Type A" personality. Hard work and achievements may have been highly valued in her family. Certainly as the oldest of five children born so closely together she would have had very little time in which to experience the mother-baby relationship. She may have had to take on responsibility for the other children early on. Finally, the mother's family myth of status made her professional attire more understandable, even though she had not come from work.

While Martha's struggles were partially the result of beliefs she had inherited from her family, Anita's struggles came from experience.

In working with Martha and Anita, as with all my clients, I suggested we look more closely at personal experience and family patterns to understand what was going on more fully. We used a tool – a genogram -- very similar to the family tree that focuses on not just ancestry but on individual personalities, belief systems, emotional health and relationships. On the following page, you'll find a simple, but dramatic example of a genogram: this one of the playwright Eugene O'Neill.

It might be helpful for you also to learn as much as you can about your great grandparents', grandparents', and your parents' experiences with suffering, disappointment, death, abandonment, etc. Just as O'Neill, you also have been affected by the beliefs, attitudes, coping mechanisms and experiences of earlier generations, as well as your own early childhood of experiences.[3] The more you understand about these, about your belief systems, the more you will understand your own identity as a person with chronic illness.

The Psalms can indeed be comforting. They speak to and from our hearts. We can picture David sitting on a rock at sunset or in the middle of the night pondering his own existence. Yet for us as for David, these thoughts raise even bigger questions. If I am to understand who I am, to make sense of my suffering I need to look deeper. I need to look into the questions that have been asked by our parents and their parents from the beginning of time.

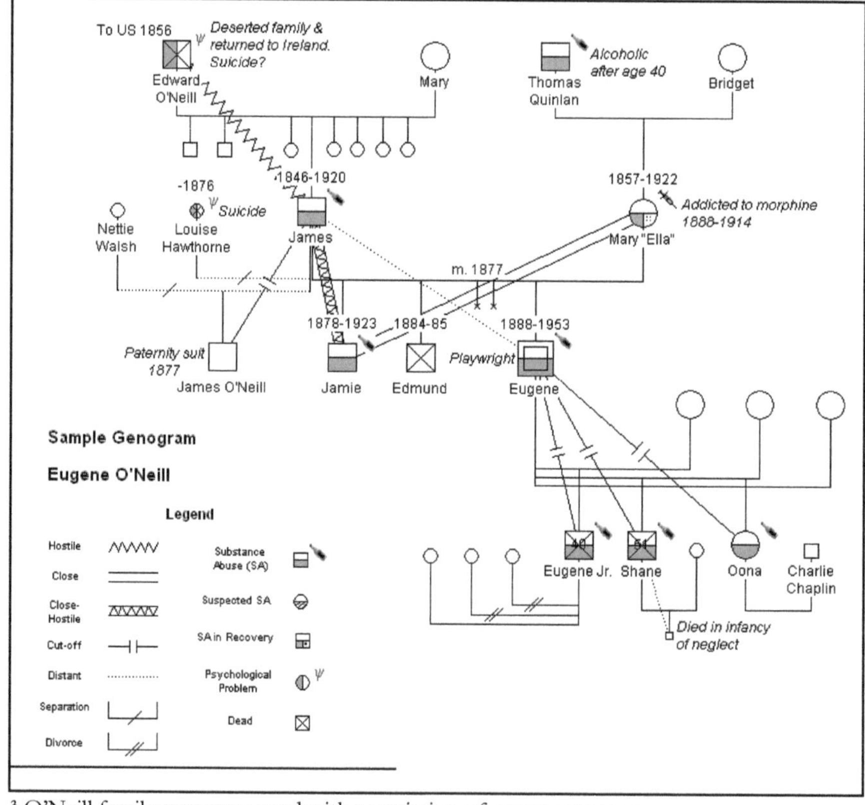

3 O'Neill family genogram used with permission of www.genogram.org

The youngest of four girls, Tina had always been athletic. Early on her father had identified her as the son he never had. With her natural ability, she relished the special attention she got from her dad. By taking the role of son, she also allowed the third child to retain the position of "baby of the family". Dad was able to relive his childhood by coaching her track team and being very involved in her basketball and soccer careers. In high school the family's weekly routine revolved around her sports. Then colleges were courting her with athletic scholarships. She was the family hero. With so much of her self-esteem and identity wrapped around physical fitness, Tina was traumatized when, at the age of 20, she began to experience extreme fatigue and muscle weakness. No matter how hard she tried, she couldn't keep up. She was becoming clumsy, unfocused and depressed. She was seen by several sports medicine specialists, given extensions on her courses, cajoled and then threatened by coaches, teammates and family.

Everyone around her was trying to get the old Tina back. She was treated for depression, given diet supplements and told it was all in her head, a sudden fear of failure. Tina did get depressed and confused. Suddenly she was no longer anybody's hero. She felt lost and abandoned and without a sense of identity. It wasn't until four years later, after losing her scholarships, dropping out of school, failing at a series of menial jobs, and finely attempting suicide that anyone suggested she might have CFIDS.

Matti has a similar story. Her physical beauty, especially her thick, shiny blond hair and translucent complexion had been her source of attention and adoration. An awful lot of confidence was wrapped up in her appearance and her ability to charm people. When at twenty-three she also began to lose weight she felt even better about herself. But weight loss was accompanied by a rash across her cheeks and small bumps on the back of her hands and on her forehead. She became too thin and her hair started to fall out in chunks. Confidence was replaced by shame. As weakness and fatigue and pain set in, Matti searched several doctors before receiving the lupus diagnosis.

While Tina and Matti had learned distorted views of their value and worth, they had been taught that problems can be solved and started looking until they found help. But what happens when life experiences and family have taught us that authorities, especially doctors can't be trusted? The bizarre array of symptoms that characterizes fibromyalgia and CFIDS can turn into a nightmare of confusion, isolation and despair. Just as problematic is the environment that validates only God's immediate and direct intervention in healing. When God does not heal and other options are withheld, the pain and suffering are exacerbated by terrible questions about sin and faith and God's love.

Katherine tossed and turned in bed for a long time before she seriously thought about getting up. Every joint in her body ached and she felt bruised all over. No position was comfortable and she was tired. As usual, the pain had kept her from really relaxing so sleep had been pretty superficial. Dressing would be an arduous chore; she would need to take breaks and rest a couple of times and all this would probably make her late for work. This morning her fingers are really swollen so it is almost impossible to button her blouse and by the time she heads for the stairs all she really wants to do is crawl back in bed. But she doesn't. She swallows a handful of prescription medications and heads to work. She will struggle through the day in pain but no one will notice. Katherine is an overachiever. For her there are no excuses.

Elise is 12 years old and brilliant, but she will not be going to school today. She is homeschooled by her parents, not out of any philosophical conviction but simply because she lacks the stamina to function in a normal school setting. So now she must struggle with isolation and abandonment by her friends who don't understand and don't want to sit with her in her pain. Mom has become her too-constant companion and so the classic mother-daughter conflicts common to twelve-year-olds are intensified and distorted. Elise is delightful but when I first met her six years ago I would not have used that term. She had the family in turmoil with her tantrums, her nightmares and her anxieties. Her frustration tolerance was minimal and she was angry. The therapy focused on behavioral management skills and reinforcement of parental authority structure. Elise calmed down. However, it was only with three years of hospitalization, visits to specialists, and several surgeries, that Elise's real problem came to light. This child had been suffering severe headaches associated with severe chemical allergies, probably since infancy. She had never said so because no one ever asked. She had just assumed that everyone hurt, that pain was part of everyone's daily life.

Alexis was diagnosed with fibromyalgia four years ago. For six years previously, she had experienced increasing muscle and joint pain and weakness. She was easily fatigued and became irritable; it was hard for her to function in her job as a nurse's aide because she couldn't lift. It was tough to function as a wife and mother of two active boys because of her fatigue and inability to concentrate. Alexis, like Katherine and Elise, was alone in her pain. She had taught her family to be "care-takers", not care givers and now that she had less to give, they resented her and refused to recognize her needs. Her husband refused to accept her illness and labeled her lazy. The boys followed his example. When Alexis needed them most, they withdrew. Her husband left her and spent a lot of time and money in an attempt to avoid any financial responsibility for a woman who is legally disabled because of an illness she didn't ask for, an illness that has cost her her career, her family, her home, her security and her self-esteem.

Each of these individuals is at a place where she needs to understand who she is in a new way. . What does it mean to be human? What does it mean to be me? Like most people, Katherine, Elise and Alexis have been taught that their value and worth comes from their ability to produce. We live in a product-oriented society. From the time we enter school we are taught that A's are better than B's, that agility and strength are better than clumsiness, that pretty is better than plain. In church we are to attend every event, be enthusiastic in our worship and inexhaustible in our evangelism. For reasons such as these, identity, the sense of who I am as a being unique and different but connected with other unique beings, is one of the most common issues in therapy. The lack of the sense of identity or a feeling that my identity is somehow wrong or invalid is one of the major causes of clinical depression.

Identity issues are frequently behind adolescent behavior problems, marital conflicts, and suicidal behavior.

If our identity is determined by our achievement then we must perform at all costs. Workaholism seems to be the only addiction that is not only condoned but applauded in our society. When I was in seminary and struggling with the prospect of being a single woman pastor with lupus, I was overwhelmed by statements from clergy who proudly declared that they put sixty to eighty hours per week into their ministries, that to do less is to fail as a pastor. I was devastated. I knew I couldn't do that. I also knew I couldn't be "up" and "on" all the time. My home and my life could not be available to anyone who wanted a piece of me all the time. I was the Type A personality. I was product oriented, I was a people pleaser and now I was condemned to fail and to displease God.

What we produce is important because it pleases people. Competence is valued because it gives others a sense of security; they can count on us. Emotional availability is important because it offers comfort. When we fall short in these areas we disappoint. When we disappoint we get negative feedback and our sense of value and worth is diminished.

Katherine, Elise and Alexis could not keep up. They tried valiantly. Katherine struggled with graduate work, a full-time ministry, and a family for ten years while her lupus remained active. For seven of those years she was plagued daily by vertigo attacks, sometimes totally disabling, until finally a stroke stopped her dead in her tracks. Yet even in the hospital she took phone calls and worked on cases. Like Katherine, Elise and Alexis pushed themselves until they fell on their faces. For Elise, at least, there was a mother to catch her. For Alexis there was no one.

I find it interesting that our society requires that buildings be handicapped accessible, that paraplegics be given electric chairs to drive themselves to market and elevator buttons are coded in braille. If you are visibly physically challenged, we will bend over backwards to accommodate your needs. But if your handicap is invisible, we call you a malingerer or worse.

Why is that? There was a time when lepers had to isolate themselves away from society and shout out a warning whenever they approached to warn others of their presence. People were afraid they might catch the leprosy. Perhaps we are afraid that we will catch whatever it is that prevents Katherine, Elise and Alexis from keeping up. Do we as a society recognize within ourselves that which is imperfect, even inadequate? Is this product consciousness and achievement orientation all a big show to hide the fallen, crippled, inadequate human that is each of us?

Most of us will never know because we will never need to ask the question. But for a fortunate minority that question will be forced upon them and they will have an opportunity to know that meaning of "adam", of being human in God's creation.

3

A THEOLOGY OF SUFFERING

No infancy and no family, no society can perfectly prepare us for coping with chronic illness. Most of us, however, meet the situation with a whole package of untapped resources, many of which we often are not aware that we possess In a fantastic example of His sovereignty, God weaves the realities of genetic makeup, our life experiences and environment to create an ever growing and changing individual. This recognition is so important. When our theology is intact and we see the Omni God at work in our lives then we with Tina and Matti can face the questions of identity and the more complex question of suffering.

While popular theology has limited our understanding of the word "adam" to a proper name, the fact is that "adam", a word borrowed from the Ugaritic term for mankind is used in that sense 500 times in the Old Testament. What is true of humanity is true of Adam and vice versa. We are told that humanity was God's final and most pleasing creation (Genesis 1:31). We're told that we were given power and authority. We were intended to be in relationship with God and one another. That's the way it was. We are also told that we, "adam" with Adam, have chosen, like rebellious children, to do things our own way and set our own rules.

The Bad News

We live in a fallen world. Part of that fallenness is experienced through broken relationships, painful negative experiences, distorted values and priorities, conflict and suffering and through illness. While life is full of the evidence of sin, it is within our personal suffering that we come to recognize our smallness and dependence.

Life hurts and we all suffer in various ways and at various times and cope in a variety of ways. But usually the pain is transitory -- a crisis, a loss, a defeat, the effects of which will linger but eventually fade and life will go on. Pain is usually something we can isolate; my arm hurts not my whole body. It is time limited and often is outside ourselves. Even in these cases we are frequently shattered and overwhelmed. We all come to a place where we question a good God who allows such pain.

The Good News

> *"Praise to the God and Father of our Lord Jesus Christ, the Father of compassion and the God of all comfort, who comforts us in all our troubles so that we can comfort those in any trouble with the comfort we ourselves have received from God. For just as the sufferings of Christ flow into our lives, so also through Christ our comfort overflows. "*
>
> I Corinthians 1:3-5

Because of the reality of Christ we are each exposed to the potential of the miraculous. These are pretty big ideas, ideas that are difficult to put into words, difficult to understand.

Suffering

Pain and suffering are real. No amount of over-spiritualizing the subject eliminates the often-relentless, debilitating nature of physical challenges. For example, consider the symptoms of the "invisible" conditions of fibromyalgia, lupus, and CFIDS. These include the following, to varying degrees and in various combinations:

- achy joints
- achy muscles
- allergies
- anemia
- anorexia
- anxiety
- blurred vision
- breathing problems
- butterfly rash across cheeks and nose
- cough
- depression
- diarrhea
- dizziness
- dry eyes
- dry mouth
- fatigue
- fever over 100 degrees F
- feverous feeling
- generalized pain
- hair loss
- headaches
- hearing disturbances
- heart palpitations
- impaired cognition
- infection proneness
- interstitial cystitis
- irritable bowel syndrome
- itchy skin
- kidney impairment
- low-grade fever
- malaise after exertion
- menstrual cramping
- migraines
- mood swings
- morning fatigue
- mouth or skin ulcers

- multiple chemical sensitivities
- muscle tenderness
- muscle twitches
- muscle weakness
- nausea
- night sweats
- nocturia
- numbness and tingling
- pain in chest on deep breathing
- painful lymph nodes
- pharyngitis
- prolonged or extreme fatigue
- rashes
- Raynaud's phenomenon (fingers turning blue or white in cold)
- restless legs
- seizures
- sensitivity to noise, smell and stress
- skin rashes
- sleep disorders
- stiffness
- sun or light sensitivity
- swelling of fingers
- swollen feeling in tissues
- swollen joints
- tachycardia
- TMJ dysfunction
- visual blurring
- worsening of premenstrual conditions

Sufferers need a theology of suffering. Our experiences need to make sense. We create such a theology automatically, all of us, often without recognizing what we're doing. For many, especially in Europe in the wake of the devastation that was World Wars I and II and again in the US during the Vietnam era, various forms of nihilism became popular. If life hurts this much then there must be no God. Or, if God did exist he must now be dead. Thus left on our own to suffer and die, we face our existence with a stoic morbidity or self-pitying indulgence.

For Hemingway and Sartre and Nietzsche, for Kafka and Heidegger this was the answer. In his book *The Courage To Be*, Paul Tillich writes: "these words reveal the other side of Nietzsche, that in him which makes him an Existentialist, the courage to look into the abyss of non-being in the complete loneliness of him who accepts the message that "God is dead." And again Tillich writes "in Kafka's novels *The Castle* and *The Trial* the unapproachable remoteness of the source of meaning and the obscurity of the source of justice and mercy are expressed in language which is pure and classical."[4]

For others, God is present but malevolent, the hellfire and the brimstone of the God of 17th Century Puritans. Or perhaps you see God more accurately in the likeness of your stern or abusive or unempathic father who disciplined with pain? Each of these variations is recognized as a legitimate theology on the nature of God. They have had names and advocates. But more importantly, they are embraced by individual Christians who have not been able to find a more meaningful or biblically accurate way of understanding their personal journey.

Perhaps this is the result of our desire to avoid the tough topics, or perhaps it is the sloppiness with which many pastors and teachers impart systematic theology. Or perhaps they taught us but we weren't listening.

While researching this topic I spent a lot of time talking with and listening to patients who daily have endured significant pain and frustration. I was surprised at how few had a solid grasp of the biblical view of suffering. I was equally amazed at the tremendous comfort an accurate theology provides.

---

[4] Tillich, Paul. *The Courage to Be.* Yale University Press, New Haven CT, 2000.

Without creating a treatise we might well explore the kind of thinking that makes the difference between triumphant endurance and despair when faced with the questions: "How do why understand my suffering in this situation? How do I understand God's love in this suffering?" These are real questions that clients and patients ask repeatedly. Our dialogue goes something like this:

BP: *Tell me about this God that you worship.*

C: *I don't know. I never thought about it.*

BP: *Well, what adjectives would you use to describe God?*

C: *He is the creator and ruler of the universe. He sent Christ to die for our sins........... He is love.*

BP: *That sounds like a creed. What do these characteristics look like? What do you mean by God is creator and ruler, for example?*

C: *Well, I guess He is all-powerful and knows everything.*

BP: *Are you saying that you believe in an Omni God, a God who is omnipresent (every place all the time), omnipotent and omniscient? A God who doesn't make mistakes, who isn't "out there" someplace, or dead or cruel? (Of course this isn't what my client was saying, not clearly anyway, but it is what I want him to say). Well, if so, you are right. The Bible teaches us that God not only created the universe but also created you and God is continually personally involved in the details of your life.*

C: *Well if that is true why did this happen to me? To my family? How can a loving God let people suffer?*

BP: *A couple of things......... how do you understand sin?*

C: *Are you saying I got sick because I sinned?*

BP: *No, I am saying you got sick because there is sin. Just as the characters in Genesis chose to live by their own rules and choices, you and I and everybody else choose "Not God's Way" a lot. God created a pure reality but by giving us power of choice he created options and allowed us to be real persons, not robots. I like to translate "sin" to "unhealthy stuff" because it seems to me, as I read Scripture, that everything that God tells us not to do is the stuff that is hurtful to somebody. We make choices. When we make wrong choices, we sin and somebody gets hurt. My mom is dying of lung cancer. She never smoked but other people smoked. Other people made choices that caused pollution but she is the one who suffers. It is a group project, a closed system, what one person chooses affects everybody else. Choices have consequences.*

C: But I don't have cancer, I have CFIDS and I have lost my job, my home and now my wife.

BP: When unhealthiness was created by human choice it was created on every level. We don't know what makes your body function poorly but it is another variation of what prevented your boss from finding some way to accommodate your illness and your mortgage holder from putting your family's welfare ahead of his profits or your wife from running out of patience and understanding. See, it's like a domino effect. The world and all its functions are just "off" and things do not reflect God's ideals.

C: But if God loves me, why didn't he protect me from all of this?

BP: Where in Scripture does it say that when we get saved we become bubble babies? Don't bother to look. I'll tell you – no place. God never promises to isolate or protect his children from the vicissitudes of life. He only promises to walk it out with us and to somehow bring some wonderful things out of it. (Romans 8: 28)

Trust me, the conversation isn't usually this clean and concise, but you get the point. The important thing is for a person in pain to begin to sense that there is order and purpose and compassion. We can handle our hurts if we see some kind of reason behind them, a valid reason. That is why women will continue to have babies, even after experiencing labor -- it seems worth it. I want my clients to be able to look with anticipation for what will be birthed out on their suffering.

Henri Nouwen first came to my attention when I was doing my clinical work at St. Peter's Hospital in Albany, NY. His book *The Wounded Healer* had a powerful impact on me. Concepts like ministering out of our own woundedness, being able to sit with others in their pain, and walking with them on their journey, have become, I hope, hallmarks of my ministry and, I wish, my life. I recommend this book to many of my chronically ill clients because it offers a framework for living in a fallen world.

In his sermon, "God's Providence", Charles Haddon Spurgeon, on the other hand, helps us develop a sense of security in God's providence. He offers us a framework which he calls Providence and he asks us to accept the fact that our lives have an order, that reality as we know it is intricate and complex and beyond our ability to comprehend. To be able to "not understand" and yet accept what comes from the hand of God allows us in many circumstances to return to the peace of the womb and thus we are provided with an inner sanctuary which will embrace us as we see our personal experience become transformed and transforming.

During the seventh century, Francois de Salignac de La Mothe de Fenelon, the Archbishop of Cambrai, functioned as spiritual adviser to several earnest Christians at the court of Louis the Fourteenth. Part of that ministry consisted of a series of pastoral letters written in response to questions and concerns expressed by the congregants.[5] My very favorite is as follows:

"I have no doubt that God considers you to be one of his friends; otherwise he would not trust you with so many crosses, sufferings and humiliations. Crosses are God's means of drawing souls closer to Himself. And these crosses accomplish his purposes much more rapidly and effectively than all of our personal efforts together. Crosses destroy self-love at its very root, down in the depths of the human spirit where we can hardly detect them. But God knows where it is lodged, and he attacks it in its greatest strongholds.

---

[5] See Fenelon, *Spiritual Letters of Fenelon.* Kessinger Publishing Co., Whitefish, Montana, 2010.

"If we have strength and faith enough to trust ourselves completely into the hands of God and follow Him wherever He leads us there will be no need of stretching and straining to reach perfection but since we are so weak in faith, and always stopping along the way to ask questions, our journey is lengthened and we get behind in spiritual development. So you see how important it is for you to abandon yourself as completely as possible to God, and continue to do so until your last breath. And don't be afraid. He will never leave you."

I must say that Fenelon's letters have been a tremendous source of comfort and peace in my own journey with pain and disability. And it seems almost as though John Wesley, eleven centuries later, wrote an addendum to this letter when he wrote his sermon "The Important Question" in which he builds a case for suffering as a positive and necessary part of the Christian experience. His reasoning is that without disappointment and pain we are unable to truly experience God's blessings. When understood from the prospective of chronic illness, Wesley, along with Fenelon and Spurgeon, is asking us to live out our illness within the guidelines set out by Henri Nouwen.

These are hard sayings, spoken by great Christians. In our day, as in theirs, few Christians want to focus on what is hard and fewer want to walk out the painful journey. But for the chronically ill, there is no choice and that provides a tremendous opportunity to experience God's love and grace within the reality of a fallen world. We are able to observe within and without the intricacies of God's plan. We are forced to be still and wait through the dark night for the Lord. We must sit in pain and even embrace it, much as Christ embraced the cross. And in all of this we have opportunities to know God and receive him, because we must be still. The ongoingness of suffering physical pain and frustration is much like a cloister where monks may go to spend their lives in contemplation and prayer.

When my client and I discussed God and sin and fallen reality, we used words and phrases to talk about things we cannot fully understand. "Things far beyond us." We were talking about God's *agape* love and learning to live in and through what that love means. Agape love is "a matter of will and of action, a free and decisive act on another's behalf, a spontaneous feeling which impels one to self-giving" (Kittel, p.45).[6]

No room here for wimpy sentiment. Agape love limits our options for self-actualization to those things that are consistent with God's will and grace. This is quiet, almost invisible heroism. Again Fenelon writes:

"Surrender consists, not in doing great, heroic deeds about which self can brag, but simply in accepting whatever God sends, and not seeking to change it (unless it is his will for it to be changed). Full surrender is full peace. If we are restless and concerned about things formerly renounced, we have not genuinely surrendered. Surrender is the source of true peace; if we aren't at peace, it is because our surrender is not complete." (p. 77)

For Elise this means giving up part of what she thought being a kid was all about. It means being creative in aloneness and tolerant of hers and other's limitations. For Matti, it means learning that she can't earn love and that she must be vulnerable to the generosity of others. It means learning to ask and sometimes be disappointed. But as you will see, they, with so many of us, have found in the losses and disappointments, as in pain itself unexpected blessings.

Finally, one last question: is there an alternative? Of course. From time to time I will browse the Internet "chat lines" set up around one illness or another, eavesdropping so to speak. There is little, though some, talk of God and peace here. And what witnessing is attempted is quickly set aside by the group. Rather, the discussions focus on new cures, the reliability of doctors, and how terrible life is. They comfort and encourage and support one another but it is all on a human level so it seems that nothing much happens. I am

---

[6] Kittel, Gerhard. *A Theological Dictionary of the New Testament.* William B. Eerdsman Publishing Company, Grand Rapids, Michigan, 1976.

reminded of Hemingway and Nietzsche and imagine the chatters sitting in the same abyss. This is the alternative.

As we embark on this journey, let us remember that at every point God is at work and available.

4

THE JOURNEY

The First Struggle --Denial by Design

What is denial?

When I was a little girl, I was convinced that one of the few uses for a little brother was as a scapegoat. A piece of pie was missing, dirt was tracked into the house, or a broken dish was discovered and my mom would always ask, "How did this happen?" And I would say "I didn't do it, Johnny did." Sometimes she would believe me over his protests, other times not. Of course, my deception was fairly obvious. The time someone had jumped from the tire swing into her garden, I blamed Johnny and Mom pointed out that Johnny was at Aunt Doris' house.

When we were children the word "denial" was associated with our attempts to avoid the natural and undesirable consequences of certain behaviors. Bil Keane, creator of the comic strip "Family Circus", makes us laugh and smile at the likes of his characters that claim innocence with the ever present "Not Me" ghosty character that is expected to take the blame for every prank and spill. "Who did it?" "Not Me." And some of us can remember Flip Wilson's character of Geraldine, who always claimed "the devil made me do it." There is an innocence and humor in such obviously transparent denial.

But I also remember seeing an old woman sitting serenely on her porch in her rocking chair, quietly knitting, seemingly totally oblivious to the men who were carrying her possessions to the sidewalk in front of this, her home since childhood, now condemned for demolition. And I once heard about the stench of a ghetto apartment where a mother continued to cuddle the infant she could not believe had died a week earlier.

This kind of denial, in many ways generated by the same naïve hope to avoid natural consequences of our own actions, the actions of others, or simply the fallenness of the world is one of the most misunderstood parts of the human journey. It is part of the lives of all of us and carries with it both protection and the seeds of destruction.

Tragedy is something that none of us are prepared to handle. In *Gone with the Wind*, author Margaret Mitchell was able to depict the role of denial and its contrasting characteristics. While Scarlett O'Hara may seem to remain oblivious to the realities of her life, if we look a little more closely we might recognize not only her awareness of impending doom but also her own helplessness to alter her fate. Denial is by definition an attempt to process a stark contrast between what we know to be true and what we wish were true instead.

Scarlett O'Hara is only one of countless attempts to help us understand more fully the complexities of this life and, of course, the role of denial in it. You see, life does that to us. Life just happens and sometimes it sneaks up on us from behind. Other times it hits us right in the face. And in either case we're not ready and we do not know how to get ready.

Even as I write this chapter,[7] my eighty-seven year old mother sits propped up in bed. She is coughing the violent cough of lung cancer. A nurse comes daily; the oxygen man will be here at 1:00. She hardly eats at all anymore. She has about two months to live. She has been told this. But Mom never smoked and Mom is not a contented person. She wants more from life than she has received and she has never trusted the future, especially death. She also has

---

[7] In November, 1998.

Alzheimer's. So now she sits trying to make a list of old friends (now dead) that she will write to and perhaps we can go visit in the spring.

Mom is in denial. We must let her be there. With Scarlett and the old lady in the rocking chair and the mother with the dead baby, Mom needs time to adjust to reality. Mom needs time to process the stark contrast between what she knows is true and what she wishes were true instead.

As reflected in such self-help groups as Alcoholics Anonymous, accountability for our own behavior involves dealing with denial. Denial keeps us from action. Denial dis-empowers us. Yet at the same time, denial gives us time. Time to absorb the importance of a challenging or devastating situation. Time to allow the first wave of emotion to pass over. Time to find ways of "normalizing" the circumstances.

.

Why is there denial?

Very simply, the human psyche can only absorb and integrate so much material in a given period of time.

Someone close to Charlie dies and suddenly he feels like he has been thrust into some parallel universe -- everything is the same but everything is somehow different. Charlie can't take it in so he removes himself from the situation. This is denial.

Maria looks away from the steering wheel for a moment and causes a serious automobile accident. When the police arrive, she knows that somehow it all must be real but at the same time hopes it's but a dream. This is denial.

The doctor returns with a gloomy report from an important medical test – Barb hears her words but something inside insists upon scrambling their meaning. This is denial.

There is a well-known story about a twelve-year-old boy who came home from school, walked through the front door, put his books down, went into kitchen to get something to eat, returned to the living room, turned on the TV and sat down. In the process he twice had to step over his unconscious father who was lying in his own alcoholic vomit in the middle of the living room. The boy couldn't deal with the fact of his father's alcoholism so he pretended it wasn't there. They call this the "elephant in the living room" story. That is denial.

How is denial connected to chronic illness?

With chronic illness, denial is an even more inevitable and necessary part of the coping process than in the sudden shock situations. After all, few chronic illnesses appear suddenly in all their full-blown glory. There are usually tell-tale signs that could be pointing to something serious, but are wished away from our consciousness in the early stages. In these cases, denial is a long-term development not just an immediate reaction to a challenge.

Certainly the slow development of chronic illness is true of the cases we're focusing on here. Remember Katherine? She had been suffering from severe vertigo attacks, several times daily for seven years, seeking help repeatedly only to be told over and over and over again that it was all in her head --a psychological problem. That is, until an extremely severe attack and an MRI exam revealed that she had been having TIAs (transient ischemic attacks), minor strokes, all this time. Ultimately, she was diagnosed with fibromyalgia and lupus as other symptoms manifested themselves...

In another case a raspy voice had appeared out of nowhere and lasted for several years, just a little worse over time until a variety of symptoms manifested a neuromuscular disease.

As I have watched these patterns in others and experienced it in my own life, I am struck by the symbolism, by the metaphor, so to speak. Our physical challenges so often reflect the broader, spiritual, cosmic challenges of life in a fallen world. Physically, we are often sick before we know it and long before we admit it. We tolerate pain as annoyance and abnormalities as inconveniences until we are forced to do otherwise.

Why? Why don't we run for medical help immediately and why do doctors look at us blankly as we share our observations? I think one explanation has to do with the complexity of the human body. It has taken centuries, millennia, for the medical community to discover how true Psalm 139 is: *"I am fearfully and wonderfully made"*. That is, the systemic intricacy and the universal mutual dependence of each particle on all the others is a work of God.

When one organ gives out the ramifications are seemingly endless. Organ failure is an all too common lupus development. Blindness can come from diabetes. It is often only when something like this occurs that one realizes the significance of a function otherwise silently taken for granted.

But we are not only complex physically. There is an unquestionable complexity in the interdependence of body, mind and spirit; in the interconnections between the physical and emotional and rational self; in how hormones secreted by our body affect our emotions which in turn affect our understanding, perception and behavior. And we come to realize that chronic illness – an ever-present and unrelenting manifestation of the current less-than-perfect condition of God's creation – is a representation of the "not-whole-ness" of the whole world. Paul tells us *"the whole creation has been groaning as in the pains of childbirth right up to the present time."* (Romans 8: 22).

Chronic illness in a fallen world

We are part of that creation and with it we experience the pain and confusion of its fallenness. When we think about or talk about sin we tend to focus on human behavior, dysfunctional relationships, war, poverty and sometimes illness. We all sin, we all know this, at least intellectually and we search to know a god who forgives and redeems. So why is it that we have trouble recognizing that like human behavior and emotional disorders, physical health is all encompassing, both in its vulnerability and in its ramifications? There is no part of the human experience that is excluded from sin, from the fallen nature of creation, from its "not-whole-ness".

Our problem in handling the challenge of a fallen world and its physical pain is not one of ignorance but one of competence. We are not competent to take these challenges in stride. After all, we are the heirs of Adam who, Genesis tells us, was created to inhabit a world without sin, without disease, without death. We were not created to tolerate and are not prepared to accept the reality of decay and imperfections. This is our curse. So we seek out coping mechanisms and one of these is denial. Like the proverbial monkeys, we see no evil, we hear no evil and we speak no evil – as long as we can.

How does this work for the chronically ill? As mentioned earlier, chronic illness usually makes its appearance subtly, even invisibly. For example, Elise may have sensed something was wrong but others, even her parents, were unaware and so failed to reflect back concern and thus invalidated any suspicions she might have been harboring.

"I really wanted comforting and soothing but I had no way of knowing if my experience was like that of other children; no way of comparing what I was feeling with what other children were feeling. Was this constant headache normal? I felt that it must be because I couldn't remember ever being without it. Even my earliest memories are clouded by the dark reality of that pain.

Perhaps others were just able to tolerate it better. But how could I as a child explain my experience, explain what I was feeling in a way grown-ups could understand? I had no words for it. I just knew I felt terrible. So I got into a lot of trouble. Because the hurt wouldn't go away I'd do things, I would be mean to my brother, I had temper tantrums and my parents would punish me and when that didn't work they took me to a therapist. And the therapist kept telling them new ways to control my behavior. But nobody ever asked why. And if they had I don't know what I would've said."

---- Elise (age 12)

For Alexis, denial was a way to keep functioning and avoid rejection.

"When my dad died, the world stopped for a moment. Someone who had been there with me was suddenly gone. There were the phone calls, the arrangements to be made. I was able to take time off from work, relatives gathered around to help and support. And then there was the wake, the funeral, and the burial. These are the rituals that society created to help me, to help us through. For death, I guess every society has a ritual, a custom. But as for my fibromyalgia, that was a different story. Things were not so clear-cut. I found myself asking, 'Are the headaches really getting worse or is it all in my head?' Even I had trouble distinguishing what was normal, what was commonplace from the abnormal. Even the doctors tended to take my complaints less than seriously. I can't blame them. After all how many of us complain about headaches and feeling tired, having trouble sleeping and maybe being dizzy, tingling in hands and feet or dry mouth. I am unable to focus. And when I told him about muscle pain and aching everywhere he was not impressed. He made me feel as though this is just part of life. But why was I crumbling under it? And then there was my family. Of course they expected me to continue to be the housekeeper, cook, and the Mom. And of course, I didn't feel I could quit my job. Neither did my husband; we needed that second income. It was all so difficult.

"I was in denial and it was made worse because there are so many plausible alternative explanations for the way I felt, for the way I feel. I'm just tired. I've been under a lot of stress lately. And the kids tell me that I'm just getting old.

Maybe I try to do too much. Maybe I'm really depressed. And I know that I just don't have time to be sick, I guess that's the biggest problem."

----Alexis (age 43)

There is a morality among us, learned in childhood that says that if you don't have a fever or aren't throwing-up that you go to school. Even medical dictionaries include a term "malingering" which means consciously pretending to be sick in order to gain attention or to avoid responsibility or some activity that we might deem to be unpleasant, usually with the claim of a lot of vague and unverifiable complaints like headaches and dizziness and muscle pain. Heartless as it may seem, Alexis, her family and her doctor all wondered if she was malingering. She had been raised with a strong work ethic. Her dad had worked every day of his life. Responsible people don't fall down on the job.

The point is that Elise, Alexis and Katherine found *they were embarking on a journey they had not chosen.* They could not clarify when they actually stepped on board or when the car began to move, or whether it was moving at all. But there they were, confused and surprised and alone and the words "this can't be happening to me" rang in their hearts like a cry for help and at the same time a final defense against reality.

Where is God as we discover our chronic illness?

"And where was God in all of this?" This is the question I so often ask at this point when my clients recall those dark cloudy days before diagnosis. The answer is often a long time in coming. For some, God wasn't even consulted because they weren't sure what to bring to Him. Others felt already betrayed and abandoned and had lost direction in their walk with God. Some, with tears, confessed that He had been their only sure thing.

Why does faith feel so difficult in times like this? For one thing the Bible says very little about the experience of chronic illness. We don't read stories about sick people, only accounts of special miraculous healings of select individuals, nothing about the course of their illnesses. Secondly, distorted theologies attempt to reconcile the "not-whole-ness" of our fallen world with the loving nature of God in various mistaken and unhelpful ways. There is the theology of "God helps those who help themselves", placing the burden upon the ill to work toward health. There is the theology (very similar to the theology of Job's friends) that states or at least implies that all illness is just evidence of personal sin, thereby placing the blame for the illness on the ill person. And there is the theology of claiming the promise that all is possible through faith – again laying the responsibility for persisting in illness upon the ill person.

All of these theologies are based on verses and parts of verses taken out of context by those who wish to live in a black and white reality because they are incapable of living in a world that God has allowed to be complex and quite often gray. Biblical theology must always consider the entirety of Scripture, not selected verses.

It is our fear of our own helplessness that leads to overly-simple theologies. By placing those who suffer in a convenient box (which we do not happen to inhabit), others are able to distance themselves from the unpleasant reality. Poor theology is also the result of inadequate Bible teaching and preaching by those who out of laziness have allowed themselves to remain ignorant. Before we try to explain the role of chronic illness in God's plan we must first be capable of careful close exegetical study of Scripture, the whole Scripture.

The time in my life in which I experienced similar vague bodily changes, fatigue and confusion was a wandering time. It was not so much the New Testament with its abundance of promise and hope but the Old Testament with its stories of the struggles of God's people with which I could identify. So many of God's people found themselves on journeys they did not understand. Abraham was told: *"leave your country, your people and your father's household and go to a land I will show you".* Moses, the Israelites, even our Lord Jesus Christ had desert experiences.

This is a time of waiting, a time to be alone. All our defenses are crumbling. Our ideas about who we are and what life, our life anyway, is all about are beginning to get fuzzy. We might be scared but we are too tired to run. We would do something but we don't know what to do, we would pray, but how? This is the time of watching our power to control our own destiny slip away.

We don't let go easily. We are strong people. And God gives us time and waits upon us. He allows us to do all we can do to keep control.

I have watched little children struggle to master a task too advanced for them, angrily fighting off any proffered assistance until tired and frustrated, they tearfully give up. Only then can Mommy come to their aid. So God waits and finally we recognize that we can't do this alone. Indeed, we were not created to be able to do this alone. We need help.

"Jeremiah 29:11 was a real source of strength to us from the beginning. 'For I know the plans I have for you', declares the Lord, 'plans to prosper you and not harm you, plans to give you hope and a future'. (NIV) We developed the habit of reciting it every morning. It provided us with a foundation. Especially when things were going badly for Elise, this daily routine kept her focused. We were encouraged by remembering that if God is who he says he is then He knows what is happening; He is not stopping it so He must be planning to use it. And we know that 'in all things, God works for the good of those who love him who have been called according to his purpose.' Elise has since developed a whole list of verses in which she finds comfort. She also journals every day."

---- Elise's mother

The Second Struggle -- -- The New Reality of Pain

Experiencing the pain

For many of us, the wake-up call comes in the form of pain. This we can't ignore and even if we can't explain it, it is real and it is tangible and in many cases unrelenting. Those who have not experienced this kind of suffering cannot fully understand how draining it is. Pain is intended by God to be a warning signal that something is wrong and needs our attention. But chronic pain does not stop. Often it does not respond to medication. We have to learn to live with it. It is a heavy load. Life slows down. Energy wanes. We are tired, often exhausted, yet we can't relax. Muscles stay taut trying to bear the load and mental energy is taken away from regular pursuits and poured into the areas of pain in an effort to cope.

"I used to kid my children that if I had known how painful childbirth was I never would gotten pregnant and if I had known how tough it was to raise three girls, I would have had boys. But when CFIDS took over my life there was no joking. I felt that my life was being taken away. My children lost their mommy and, for the most part, my husband lost his wife. The total exhaustion of CFIDS was like nothing I had experienced. It hurt. It hurt so much that when I wasn't tired I was afraid, really afraid of being tired. Of course my family couldn't understand though they tried. It was very lonely."

-- Rachel, age 38

"My son looked at me like I was nuts the first time I asked him to pour the breakfast cereal for me. He couldn't believe that it hurt me to do that. I have great kids and a great husband but the pain was all mine. As a family we shared my illness but they couldn't, they can't take the pain away. It is there 24 hours a day, no matter what I do or don't do. It has been there for twelve years."

-- Becky, age 33

Embracing the pain and disability

We don't have to be heroes or martyrs. As children, we probably whined and cried like all the other children. But early on we learned that we can either allow pain to run our lives or we can find ways around it. Sometimes that just meant using crutches; other times later on in life it might mean moving to a one-story house or changing careers.

The summer after my first year in seminary I had the opportunity to do mission work in Africa. It had been a marvelous experience; very dramatic, reinforcing all those images I had developed listening to the stories, watching the films and the slides of seasoned missionaries back home on leave when I was a child. But while I was there I also got African tick bite fever. This is a very serious disease and in Africa, at least where I was, the custom is to not treat it because if you survive it you'll never get it again. Upon my eventual return to America I resumed living home with my parents while I continued my work at seminary. Soon after my return my parents split up.

It is amazing how our feelings as adults in such matters are so like those of children. Since I was living at home this was more traumatic for me than perhaps it would've been otherwise. The situation at home bled into my enthusiasm over my experience in Africa. The hours of classes and study quickly became an impossible escape from my feelings. Every lesson and every lecture was now painfully tainted with the personal reality of what a fallen world we live in. As the weeks went by and life fell into a pattern, unpleasantness seemed to contaminate every area of life. This emotional stress coupled with the physical trauma of the tick bite fever began to affect me physically and I developed a rash: hard to disguise, hard to explain. People began to ask if I was ill.

In the morning I would awaken with stiff and painful joints and that made it hard to rise in shine with the joy of the Lord. Odd bumps of coagulated tissue would appear painfully and then disappear. At times I could hardly walk without a cane. It was hard to carry my books, let alone be perky about it. It was hard to concentrate on my studies. It was hard to hold a pen with swollen fingers. Life became gradually inconvenient and then nearly impossible. Continuing the daily and weekly routines of school and home responsibilities, I'd try to minimize the increasing pain and weakness. Getting into the car, sitting up, eating, all became exhausting tasks. Sleep became a distant memory as muscle and joint pain made the slightest movement intolerable. For months the disease progressed largely unrecognized. Most of my symptoms, except the rash, I could cover-up pretty well. Then I continued to lose weight, my hair began to fall out and my gums started to bleed. The slightest bump would cause a major bruise. Eventually, I couldn't study because I couldn't focus my eyes. I couldn't attend class because I was too weak to dress. There was no longer any way to hide it, I was very sick.

I was taken to doctors who looked puzzled and concerned and who gave lame diagnoses like rheumatoid arthritis and sent me home with aspirin. What was going on? Was this also part of my adventure? My family and friends pondered with me silently the meaning of suffering. All the traditional questions were asked: "Who sinned, the boy or his parents?" … "Why do bad things happen in good people?" … "If you had enough faith this wouldn't have happened." Bargains were made with God.

By the time the lupus had developed to a point where it became my life, I was asking fewer questions than anyone else and I felt no need to bargain. In the hours and weeks that turned into months and seasons, I began to experience my time in the wilderness where the pain and I became great friends. I discovered that pain can be embraced and welcomed. In those dark alone hours between one and four a.m. when the world is asleep, pain is there, almost indistinguishable from one's own identity. One can crawl inside its warmth as into a womb, where self and non-self intermingle. One can numb it by hyperventilating.

Pain would draw me away from the details of daily life to a place somewhere between heaven and earth. God was there and all life was at once simple and extremely complex. Everything was acceptable and made sense. The Omni God was very personal and very, very safe. The concrete and the spiritual became the extremes on a continuum, along which I and all humanity constantly migrated.

Lessons in theology had new meaning and long memorized verses had new depths and Christ was confronted face-to-face on a daily basis. If the "Holy Hill" of the seminary had been a womb-like experience then pain and darkness became the second. If a chance to minister in Africa had been the first adventure, then this solitary vigil became the second. Enthusiasm and energy now gave way to confident acceptance of whatever came from the hand of God.

"I can't believe how grateful I am for all that I have learned, not for the pain itself but for what it did for me. I am so much more aware of who I am. I have had to develop creative ways to live my life because my body hurts so much. I am young. I don't want to be unhappy all the time so I find nice things that I probably wouldn't even notice otherwise. And I listen more."

-- Wendy, age 24

<u>Growing through the pain</u>

I believe that every one of us can grow through the pain that God permits us to endure. I sometimes feel that God is very area precise and efficient in his mentoring. Looking back it seems as though I was repeatedly given opportunities, like some celestial homework assignment: "Here is your situation. What do you see? What can you discover?" The Africa project had been a lesson in obedience, yes, but more so a lesson in the complexity and the solid reality of spirituality that supersedes and colors all intellectual understanding. This new adventure was a journey into that reality, beyond what intellect and reason can communicate, that existential confrontation with God that is very personal and cosmic at the same time, the kind of adventure that probably led others to the great metaphors and symbols of the Bible:

"I am a fighter. I always have been. Even literally. I boxed my way through college and graduate school. And it took me years to realize that I couldn't fight this pain and win. It was a great metaphor for my Christian life as well. Finally I learned to let go. I learned relaxation exercises. I replaced boxing with Tai Chi and centering exercises. My life is much quieter now. It is a warm place to be. I think my family likes me better this way."

--Bill, age 27

There is something about ongoing intense pain that challenges the soul when one faces the possibility and the likelihood that life and pain will be synonymous from now on. There is the transformation and re-appraisal of priorities. Textures and sounds and slants of light, the comforting sounds of conversations far away, the minutes that expand into timelessness. Most of all there is "being" for when one can no longer "do". Then there is nothing left but to be; to be still and know God. I am not being super-spiritual or dramatic by using such language. I felt and continue to feel so grateful for being allowed to wander in that place. That wilderness was my opportunity to wander in the desert with Moses and study theology with Paul and even fast there with Christ. To think that God is that generous to us normal folk in all our shallowness and superficiality. It is as though God accepts and delights in accepting us as we are and challenges us to be more than we are by sharing His secrets, His very being with us.

As a counselor and therapist, I find that my clients heal and grow more from the experience of the therapeutic experience itself than from any technique or applied theory. It is the consistently attuned, empathic and trustworthy holding environment that allows the self to "be" and "become". If such miracles occur through human vessels, what are the glories of being so held by God?

The Third Struggle -- -- The Search for a Diagnosis

No answers

Diagnosis can be one of the most difficult and frustrating aspects of medicine. Incorrect diagnosis can be at the very least an annoyance and can possibly be fatal. Especially with chronic illness and especially with these three chronic illnesses – lupus, fibromyalgia and CFIDS. One looks at a list of their symptoms and it is evident why diagnosis can be confusing. Often doctors are not able to differentiate out a clear diagnosis and therefore conclude that the patient has a combination such as fibromyalgia and lupus.

Elise is an excellent example of this. She had to struggle with her own frustration over numerous doctors who threw up their hands and walked away. Like so many patients, Elise's family took matters into their own hands. With the prayer support of friends and family they did their own research and sought out specialists until they found someone who could help. What has been so significant about each of the women in this chapter is that in all the years I have known them I have never seen them give in, give up, get cynical, or wallow in negativity. In some cases, family and friends have faithfully supported them in prayer and in love. Unfortunately, while these personal characteristics are common to many fibromyalgia, lupus, and CFIDS patients, the latter is not true of their families and they have to struggle for the diagnosis and for support alone and therefore usually are not as successful as these.

Elise's story

The love and holding that surrounded Elise throughout the years was clearly an essential part of her recovery. But the way the church surrounded and encouraged her parents was equally necessary. While belonging to a church that included services of prayer and healing and which believed in God's power of miraculous intervention, Elise and her family never felt put under condemnation because of Elise's long battle with a conglomeration of illnesses that goes on to this day. It is clear that this acceptance and the ability of the church to walk alongside the family throughout this journey have been very important. While God can and does at times choose to intervene miraculously through the ministry of His church, we are way out of line when we raise ourselves to a place where we think we can determine when and how that will occur. What is sure is that the love of Christ in the Church has within it restoration powers.

Elise's mother:

"In the early years of Elise's illness, the stress was overwhelming. She seemed hyperactive, angry and violent and I had no answers. I assumed, with my background in education, that we were dealing with some trauma that came out of the infant-mother relationship. And yet I couldn't find her fitting into any pattern. At the same time her older brother was acting out his own frustrations which we learned later were the result of his superior intelligence but at that time we did not know this, we had not had him tested.

"My husband was away a lot and while he was verbally very supportive I was not able to receive his support. I got into counseling myself and I put our son in counseling. It was at that point that he was tested and was put into an appropriate school situation. This solved one of our problems but even this wouldn't have happened without the encouragement and suggestion of a dear Christian friend. While my own counseling gave me an outlet for my feelings and it helped me clarify my own understanding of what was going on, it became clearer and clearer that Elise and I did in fact have problems. My counselor and I worked very hard on improving my portion of the mother-child relationship and things calmed down for a while.

"Then Elise was out of control again and we put her into counseling. She was diagnosed as hyperactive, as being oppositional-defiant disordered, and the counselor worked on parenting skills with me while she tried to work on ferreting-out some deep rooted trauma behind the behavior. When it was clearer

that this was not helping, both therapists and I felt totally depleted. We turned to our Christian family as we never had before and it was then that we began to listen to Elise. As she tried to lead us to the truth as best she could, a series of medical diagnoses beginning with sinus disorders were pursued and to the degree that we were accurate they helped, but to the degree that there was still something wrong our journey continued for the next six years."

The importance of the supportive environment is evident in any support group or online chat room. Eavesdropping on either leaves one with the clear sense of the rage and despondency that develop when one is emotionally abandoned by family and friends. Yet one is less aware of those who, faced with the same abandonment, find Christ. They are less visible because they are usually not in chat room's seeking solace, venting anger or trying to find answers. They aren't visible unless we seek them out.

This is exactly what I discovered over the years as I conducted structured surveys of individuals with chronic illness. They have shared their thoughts and feelings regarding chronic illness and spirituality. A few responses were full of generalized anger. But over and over again the comments were wonderful as these individuals, coping with all the pain and complexities of illness took the time and made the effort to share with me their journey through Christ. Though some could hardly write their messages were clear. Christ was there for them and that had transformed their tragedy to joy. While they were rarely able to expound on this in depth, a few could talk about calm through the aloneness of the night as they recalled the memorized Scripture, the hope they felt in prayer, and the distinct way they experienced God's answers to those prayers.

Patience justified

At some point in my case, whether because the lesson was learned, the project complete or the flow of circumstance ready, things began to happen. Christians had been praying and, of course, offering their advice much like Job's wise counselors. Two parents already under stress and unable to support one another were desperate. Absolutely desperate. And there seemed to be no help and no doctor seemed to want to get involved. They just kept referring around in circles. Then one day in the summer of 1978 the phone rang and a strange woman, a friend of a friend was on the line. She had heard of my family's predicament through a prayer chain and it sounded familiar. She knew someone else with similar symptoms and referred us to a specialist at Peter Bent Brigham Hospital in Boston. My mother phoned and was given an appointment three weeks away. Hope! But the fever that had been there from the beginning was rising frightfully high, breathing was becoming labored, the odor of sickness was everywhere and evidences of paranoia and delirium were beginning to appear. I didn't want to risk further rejection by annoyed doctors if they pressed for a more immediate appointment but finally fear overcame fear and a second phone call was made. Now with a clearer picture of the symptoms, the doctor himself was consulted and he told my parents to bring me in immediately.

I remember lying in the back of my dad's car as they fought traffic and argued, frustrated and fearful, feeling as though time was running out. I too was feeling as though time was running out but I wasn't frightened or frantic. It all seemed appropriate and easy. It was just too bad I couldn't help those two people in the front seat to understand. The doctor to which we had been referred was the international authority on lupus. He said that our fears had been warranted; in another day or so and death would have probably been a reality. At the same time he was confident and excited by such a "pure and untouched example" because no one had really tried to treat my symptoms and because I was so sick that I exhibited all the right symptoms in magnificent clarity. But life being as it is and medical priorities being what they are, he had to save the life and prescribed the medications before he could photograph all the evidence. That was really too bad.

That next morning, a troop of third year medical students marched into the small hospital room with faces masked and notepads in hand ready to analyze the specimen. Much to the doctor's chagrin, there sat before them, cross-legged, perky, full of energy and very hungry, a bright-eyed bushy-tailed and exquisitely skinny female. It was a disappointing day for them but while it wasn't all photographable, we did add substantially to the understanding and treatment of the disease. That was kind of a nice place to be but it was even nicer to learn that while when I get sick, I get very, very sick, I also respond very, very well to most medications. Thus began another adventure.

The Fourth Struggle -- Grieving Our Losses

Alexis's story

Week after week, Alexis came to my office in tears. Yes she hurt all over and the migraines had caused her to have to re-schedule her appointment twice but it was not the pain, nor the confusion that troubled her now. It was the losses.

"Bobby, I just can't stop crying. I just keep thinking, it seems like there's nothing left. I never thought it would be this way. I really don't know what's happening. I just can't understand what I've done to deserve this. My friends, the church, people I've known for so long, people I've trusted, people I've loved, are disappearing. My brother and his wife, even my mom, are getting annoyed with me. They say I ask too much. That I am too needy and I need to stand on my own two feet. They just don't understand. Even Bill and the kids treat me like a hired maid. All they want are their clothes washed, and meals ready whenever they decide to get there. I just can't do it; I just can't be taxi and laundry maid and cook anymore. And when Bill comes home expecting a warm greeting and a hot meal and, I have to admit, instead finds a cranky wife and an empty table, he threatens to leave for good. Now. When I need him most. They just don't help. They just don't understand. I don't know what I'd do without Bill. I couldn't manage alone. Not now." [In fact, Bill did leave for good.] But you know Bobby, that doesn't even feel like the worst of it. I just know my life will never be the same. Here I am turning 40 and I have nothing to look forward to. All the things I've wanted to do, all my dreams, all

the things I've put off to be responsible, for the kids, for the family -- like going back to college, like traveling -- there are so many things that I want to see. I really wanted to provide for my parents when they got old, I always thought that was right. I always wanted them to be in my home when they could no longer take care of themselves. I thought Bill and I would grow old together, caring for the grandchildren. I may never see my grandchildren. That's just so sad, that's just so sad, and no one understands or even seems to care."

Dreams of what might be are just as important for our sense of wellbeing as are the more tangible parts of our reality. They give us a sense of hope. They help us put into concrete terms our values; they remind us of why we're putting up with the current struggles, of why "life is worth living". For Alexis, hope was very important. She needed something to hold onto. She needed something to help her get out of bed and struggle through each day.

George's story

"I remember I was sitting in my car at a traffic light, right there in the middle of the street when all of a sudden I just started this uncontrollable crying. I'm not a crybaby. I never was. I'm usually able to handle things. But this time I couldn't even catch my breath. I couldn't figure out how to drive. I was just sitting there, bawling like baby, and blocking traffic. Here I am, an eight-year veteran of lupus but this news came out of the blue. You see, the doctor, he said I had renal failure, that means kidney failure. That is serious. That was a week ago. I don't know, I've always been able to take every setback with a kind of "can do" attitude, and that's how I was handling this one. Then all of a sudden I fell apart."

Life is full of losses. We grow, we become, we move ahead. But with each new life phase, with each new opportunity we must leave something, somebody behind. For the most part, we are able to predict our losses. But there are always surprises, there are unexpected deaths or moves and we grieve. For many of our losses, our culture has provided us with rituals to help us express our grief and fear. But there are also the private losses for which we have no rituals and perhaps no words. That is where George finds himself. Hardly able to clarify in his own mind what this vague news really means, he's certainly isn't able to talk about it. But he knows it will not be easy. It means more complications, more changes for himself and his family and probably it means that he is getting sicker.

No room at the inn

How, where and when we express our grief are important but the equally important question is to whom we express it. How many people do we have in our lives that are able and willing to, time and time again, walk out our grief with us?

There was no room at the inn for the birth of Christ, largely because the wishful theology of the day that expected the Messiah to come as an all-conquering warrior. There was little room for His arrival as a helpless infant in the mess of a stable. In the same way today, even strong Christian family members and friends have no room for the drudgery – the mess -- of relating to someone with chronic illness, wishfully preferring God to give us easy relief so that we all can get on with our lives.

Close family and friends, those who function as caregivers, bear their own pain with each successive decline. How much do they have left for us? Those on the outer perimeters of our lives often can't relate or understand and may not want to be involved. The professionals, no matter how well intentioned, are, of course, professionals. This is their job; they deal with it every day and then go home at night, hopefully, leaving George and all the other patients or clients "at the office". So George and Elise and Alexis are left alone.

But what losses are we talking about? Not just physical loss. There is so much more. Life becomes complex and things most of us take for granted become trials. Illness and medication have visible effects so every look in the mirror can be threatening and this affects self-image. But for people like George, self-image deteriorates as one's ability to hold a job and support a family are jeopardized. And what about when a provider becomes a burden? For some, the risks are greater than for others, as when needed medical treatment is not covered by insurance or is refused by the HMO. Grief and anxiety become constant characteristics of daily life. But along with these tangible and less tangible losses comes one that probably surpasses all the others -- loss of friends. Both within the family and beyond it those with whom we shared our lives begin to move away. Perhaps they cannot tolerate our pain or are annoyed that we are less capable of meeting their needs or expectations. Perhaps we're not fun anymore.

Surrounded by people, George and others like him face a dim and uncertain future. Gradually the Book of Job begins to sound more familiar and the patient relates to the man sitting among the ashes covered with boils. Well-meaning friends sound more and more like Eliphaz, Bildad, and Zophar. Even pastors pour hot oil on their wounds. It is therefore appropriate that George like Job should cry out, "*I am weary of living. Let me complain freely. I will speak in my sorrow and bitterness.*" (Job 10:1) or "*Why me, O Lord? Why have you turned your back on me?*" Or to even turn his back on God in anger and despair.

Job's friends came in good faith, appealing to his orthodoxy and faith. With their long-winded discourses they tried to fix and then to understand their friend's predicament but there was no room in their theology for Job, no cubbyhole that would fit. So they ended up frustrated and the friendship seemed to crumble as Job faced God directly. George will experience the same frustration and disappointment. His friends will come with Bible verses and prayers. But then when he doesn't get better many of them will become frustrated or lose interest. We are a quick-fix society -- "get better or get lost". Others will hang in there, helping with the daily life tasks, perhaps sitting and listening to George and even sharing his pain. These will in fact grieve with him until he is done grieving. But even with this support George will have to meet God directly, in the dark hours of the night, alone.

Already, vulnerable and beaten down, exhausted by the physical demands of his illness and their extra time consumption, the sick person is naturally going to cling to those people and places which have provided sanctuary throughout his life. But often he is turned away and even if allowed physical entrance, he is emotionally locked out or condemned. Job's friends may have used different language but the messages were the same. There is and always has been an anti-grief ideology that distorts Scripture to accommodate the insecurities of the professors. Isaiah 53: 5 and John 15:7 are verses that often subjected to such are abuse.

> *"He was pierced for our transgressions, he was crushed for our iniquities; the punishment that brought us peace was upon him, and by his wounds we are healed."*

> *"If you remain in me and my words remain in you, ask whatever you will and it will be given you."*

Certainly, the Bible is full of reminders of our grounds for rejoicing and of the centrality and power of Christ in our lives. And we are urged especially by Paul to take these seriously, *"For we are God's workmanship, created in Christ Jesus to do good works, which God prepared in advance for us to do."*(Eph.:2:10) But I don't believe that those who use such references as Isaiah 53:5 or John 15:7are intent on hurting anyone. And they truly believe that their admonitions are of God. But if we'd look at these verses in their contexts we recognize that they have a deep and more spiritual meaning, not prescribing verses for physical illness. We all look for a way to understand illness, pain and suffering. For some, taking these verses out of context seems to provide a quick solution.

But such black and white thinking leaves no room for the empathy and compassion that are so much of what Christ conveys. Therefore the patient must not only sometimes find, but also teach a theology of grieving. Such a search might well begin with Christ. Clearly here we have the God incarnate who *"took up our infirmities and carried our sorrows"* (Isaiah 53:4). He wept openly over the death of his friend Lazarus and the suffering of his sisters. He mourned all that Jerusalem might have been and wasn't. (John 23:37). He was able to confront disciples who still did not understand the meaning of his life and death. (John 14)

All of our theology, the answers to all of our questions must begin with Christ. Who and what he was and is, and this must inform our understanding of the rest of Scripture. If we look at Paul or Isaiah or read Genesis -- touch any of the Scriptures without first recognizing Christ as the foundation and core of our faith and of the Bible -- we're likely to misunderstand and distort God's intended message.

As with all else in God's creation, emotions have a purpose. *("There is a time to weep and a time to laugh, a time to mourn and a time to dance."* Ecc 3:4). They can be used and misused. Honest grieving cleanses the soul. It eventually washes away the pain and allows us to move forward. Mourning is a time for working out and working through the crisis of loss and change, to find our new identity in this new kind of living. This mourning humbles us. We come face to face with our human frailty and our need for God's grace and thus prepare the way for God's work in us to finally lift the veil of a transition to a new reality.

The Fifth Struggle -- What Constitutes A Miracle?

The Problem of Suffering and Loss

The greatest problem with pain and suffering is that it flies in the face of all that we understand about Justice. Recall that we discussed that being created in God's image gives us an unavoidable determination to see all things in terms of right and wrong, fair and unfair. As Christians in particular we ask questions: "how can God allow such things happen to good people?" A careful look at Scripture reveals a record succinct explanation.

First of all human suffering, including but not limited to sickness and death, was not part of God original plan. God's plan was one of goodness and perfection but he also intended that the creatures who were to bear his damage have the power of free will (Genesis 3:15 -- 18). The phrase "knowledge about good and evil" is an idiom for, or a synecdoche for "all things, everything". In other words, when the first beings are said to disobey this command they were seeking to be "all knowing", to be God. God does not include this story simply to explain death and suffering in some prehistoric tale of the origin of things. He is not as concerned about epistemology as to show us a true reality we live out each day. As individuals and as nations we choose our own wisdom over the precepts of God, over the righteousness of God. We have been doing this for millennia. The consequences are seen in fish born in and our ponds without fins, in dwindling rain forests, in Colombian drug tycoons and fifth graders bullying classmates into suicide.

In the book of Job, we have the fullest explanation of the causes of suffering of the "good man". In the midst of his pain and grief, in the presence of friends who primarily want to fit Job's circumstances into the cubicles of their theological orthodoxy for their own comfort, Job refuses the same rationalizations the sick hear all the time. "Who sinned, this man or his parents?" The answer is neither and both. Sometimes we do reap the consequences off our own sin. If I smoke cigarettes, I will probably get cancer and I really can't blame anyone else. But sometimes the cause of my suffering clearly belongs to another, as in the case of crime victims. But more often our illnesses, especially, are the results of eons of fallenness and corruption and decay that have over centuries changed our world at the sub-molecular level. (Luke 13: 1 - 5)

God never promised to put a bubble around any of us. We all sin and we all experience the consequences of sin, our own and others, even as Christians but He does promise to walk it out with us. And as Christians, to bring something positive out of it. For

> *"not only so, but we also rejoice in our sufferings, because we know that suffering produces perseverance, perseverance, character; and character, hope".*
>
> (Romans 5:3 -4).
>
> *"That the creation itself will be liberated from its bondage to decay and brought into the glorious freedom of the children of God. We know that the whole creation has been groaning as in the pains of childbirth right up to the present time. Not only so, but we ourselves, who have the first fruits of the Spirit, groaning inwardly as we wait eagerly for our adoption as sons, the redemption and of our bodies. For in this hope we were saved.*
>
> *"But hope that is seen is no hope at all. Who hopes for what he already has? But if we hope for what we do not yet have, we wait for it patiently. In the same way, the Spirit helps us in our weakness.*
>
> *"We do not know what we ought to pray for, but the Spirit himself intercedes for us with groans that words cannot express.*
>
> *"And he who searches our hearts knows the mind of the Spirit, because the Spirit intercedes for the saints in accordance with God's will.*
>
> *"And we know that in all things God works for the good of those who love him, those who have been called according to his purpose."*
>
> (Romans 8:21-28)

Here, we should probably address the problem of faith. Too often my clients have been berated by pastors for their lack of faith in the midst of their suffering, being told that if they only had enough faith God would heal them.

This is a blatant misinterpretation and misuse of Scripture. A careful, close exegetical look at what the WHOLE BIBLE says about miraculous healing reveals that miraculous healing, like all other miracles are intended for the specific purpose; namely that those present and we who read should be pointed toward God. It is as though God chooses to pierce through their reality of time/space like a huge fist punching through the clouds to reveal God's glorious face. God does not pick favorites. He desires of us that we all know him, his love and his truth. When we pick out a verse here and a verse there to support some idea we want to believe and find comfortable, we inevitably end up with distortion and pain. As Christians we are assured of being held and comforted in the midst of our suffering

> *"Who shall separate us from the love of Christ? Shall trouble or hardship or persecution or famine or nakedness or danger or sword?*
>
> *As it is written:*
>
> > *'for your sake we face death all day long; we are considered as sheep to be slaughtered'*
>
> *No, in all these things we are more than conquerors through him who loved us."*
>
> (Romans 8: 35 -- 37)

We are also given the opportunity to use our experience in glorifying God through a closer more dependent relationship

> *"Before I was afflicted I went astray, but now I obey your word."*
>
> (Psalm 119: 67)

"Be still, and know that I am God;

I will be exalted among the nations,

I will be exalted on the earth."

(Psalm 46: 10)

Of course, we can always wallow in our pain, whine and curse God. Or we can, like Job, hold steadfast and allow God to be God, whereby we rest in God's hands, seeking to understand his will and our role in bringing about this will.

"You said, 'Listen now, and I will speak;

I will question you, and you shall answer me.'

My ears had heard of you but now my eyes have seen you."

(Job 42: 4 - 5)

<u>Waiting to be zapped</u>

Have you ever seen a miracle? That is what George is looking for. In those dark hours of the night when he is alone with his anxiety and pain, he waits and hopes that God will speak, that God will do something. But what? George, like a so many of us, is looking for some magic intervention, a miraculous healing -- "Zap" and he is suddenly healed. In some ways George's theology is good. He seeks an intervention by God and in fact a careful study of Scripture indicates that all miracles are God's intervention in the normal functioning of our reality. God punches through reality with His fist, He reaches into us from His existence beyond time and space, from a reality beyond our comprehension.

When we read the Old Testament, we see God acting, but always on behalf of the Jews. In the New Testament, Jesus healed the sick but not everyone, only a certain few. But what about all the others who were sick? What about all the other nations of the world? Don't they too deserve the magic of God? That is what George is asking tonight, "What about me, God?"

But George's theology is off track here. Its answer to the "Why" question is wrong. God's miraculous intervention in the laws of nature, His interruption of our reality is never for the welfare of any one person. Yes God does loves that person but He loves all of us. He wants all of us to know Him. As recorded in Scripture and in our present-day God's miracles are for the sole purpose that we might see Him. Always, always, always God is calling all mankind to know Him.

So as long as George seeks a Santa Claus-like God, God will never be present to him. His ears may have heard of him, but the "eyes" of his soul (to paraphrase Job 42) will never see him.

Samuel Beckett, an Irish playwright of the Theater of the Absurd, an anti-establishment literary movement of the early twentieth century, in 1953 wrote a short two-act play called "Waiting for Godot". It is about two men who sit on a park bench waiting for someone named Godot. Godot never comes. The men leave the stage and the audience is left to wonder who Godot might be? What is the point of this empty play? Is Godot God? Is Beckett questioning the existence of God? Do we question, dare to question whether God is, and if He is, then where is He now when I need Him?

George is in the same position. God is there but he can't see Him because he is looking for something spectacular. In waiting for a miraculous recovery George is not truly able to say "not my will, but thine be done".

God's grace in our suffering

Sharon is in a very similar position. Her ailments had not responded to medication and now her symptoms seemed to be on the rampage, rendering her almost incapable of any normal functioning. She also went through anger and grieving and fear. She also has her alone time in the dark hours of the night. But her faith and her understanding of Scripture had brought her further than George had come. Early on she discovered that shallow breathing assuaged her pain and cramping and in that mode, a numbness came upon her; the world felt far away. She was alone while humanity slept. Yet there was a presence. She could not move for fear of the pain such activity could and would bring. She was still, the night was still. In those hours she learned the blessing of "being" instead of "doing", the piece of meditation and the joy of waiting on the Lord. The verse that she remembers and thought about more than any other was Psalm 37:3-5:

> *"Trust in the Lord, and do good;*
>
> *So you will dwell in the land, and enjoy security.*
>
> *Take delight in the Lord*
>
> *And He will give you the desires of your heart.*
>
> *Commit your way to the Lord;*
>
> *Trust in Him and He will act."*

In that quiet and in that peace, she became aware of a presence with her. Not in clashing symbols nor with trumpets, but with warmth and unbelievable calm: "a peace that passes all understanding". And suddenly everything was all right. Whatever was to come from the hand of God was acceptable. Her greatest fears of death and abandonment now seemed irrelevant. Sharon was now free to see God work in her life and use her and her illness to His glory. Her prayer was not "heal me" but "use me". And that was the beginning of a lifetime of miracles, large and small, that allow others to see God.

Like Sharon, I also have experienced the wonder of seeing God working in and through me. After all, lupus is not one of the diseases you get over. Rather it becomes a part of who you are. I have seen people try to fight the disease, resenting the impact it is having on their lives. I have seen others easily defeated, perhaps feeling isolated and hopeless. Their lives become a series of complaints and they lose their capacity for wonder and joy. I find this to be very sad and I believe it to be a choice. In a society that encourages quadriplegics to do their own errands on motorized wheelchairs, we as Christians should be the first to see life as full of challenges instead of disabilities.

This is not intended to be a judgment, rather an observation about attitude. Our attitudes develop slowly over time, through experience seasoned with the subtle influences of those around us. Our feelings combine with our thoughts and emerge as reason; experience and reason collide and form our attitudes.

Most of the time we live our lives in response to these attitudes, these assumptions which we have absorbed like a sponge absorbs water, heavy and full, having lost the capacity for further possibility. Unlike the sponge, you and I are capable of choice. Especially through our faith and the Lord working in our lives, we have the option to expect and accept wonders and surprises. Dale Evans Rogers wrote a book titled *Angel Unaware.* Even without going beyond the title, one is confronted with the miraculous that awaits each of us, no matter our circumstance, if we so choose.

So many clients and parishioners have asked in times of suffering, "Why me?" And my answer is always the same. God never puts a bubble around His children to protect them from the fallenness of this world. We do suffer. No one is exempt. But God does walk it out with us. He does provide respites. There is always meaning and purpose to be discovered (not imposed). And there is always an end.

In my case, a rapid-acting medication (known as prednisone) put my family and me into a kind of natural high. Relief from pain produces its own high. But the euphoria had to give way to practical considerations. First of all, I had to gain weight (boy do I wish someone would tell me that today). I still remember the once-in-a-lifetime opportunity that came a week after I was released from the hospital. I went into our local Friendly 's Ice Cream Shop and ordered and ate, all by myself, a huge chocolate sundae with coffee ice cream with marshmallow, whipped cream, nuts, and sprinkles, and no guilt -- after all these years to remember that time with real joy!

Life was good but it was also becoming complex. I was on a regimen of several medications, each supporting or compensating for another. Wellness was now a matter of balance. Enough medication to suppress symptoms but no more than absolutely necessary in order to minimize negative side effects. While pill-taking became routine it has unfortunately made me less than sensitive to those who whine about an ache or pain but refuse to take an aspirin for fear of its effects. I guess I believe that if God in his wisdom saw fit to enable us to discover and create medications, we can assume He intends for us in our wisdom to use them.

But even medications are not the panacea we often want them to be. Joint pain, sensitivity to the sun, tiredness and weakness were always present. I was extremely vulnerable to every cold and virus around. I carried Maalox in a flask and chugged it like the most dedicated drunk and considered the telltale 'white mouth' to be a normal part of my new look. It went well with the "sensible" shoes, though they often got traded for heels that hurt (oh, the power of vanity). Makeup often did not hide the rashes and the bruises that became permanent. Even now, whenever I go into the hospital or see medical personnel unfamiliar with my history or with lupus, I need to carefully explain my odd appearance because they misunderstand it for evidence of physical abuse.

Long sleeve shirts and slacks quickly replaced sundresses and shorts in the hot summer sun. This was long before society in general began to turn its back on the suntanned look. It's nice to be a trendsetter; too bad blue and green never really made it as a popular alternative. Then there was the hair loss. Did you know that sometimes medication can have side effects that are almost identical to the symptoms they are treating? Yes, hair falling out in chunks and thinning continually became an issue. (And this was before Rogaine.)

It has all been one real lesson in vanity for someone who began life as an adorable Shirley Temple who was carried around restaurants by waitresses. Appearance had always been a source of anxiety for me. For decades I had been trying to earn acceptance through beauty and charm. Now I had to either pack it all in or wear a bag over my entire being for the rest of my life. That seemed to risk a lot of unwanted attention so I decided to give in. It's amazing how effectively God gets us right where we hurt and right where we need it. He was going to deal with this superficial orientation once and for all.

When a 'flare' would come, steroids increased, pain decreased but then I was left with the "moon face" which again drew attention. 'Yesterday you looked normal and today you look like Porky Pig with lipstick.' You can imagine how all this affected my popularity; not positively, but I did get attention.

I became a project. My illness became a learning experience for a certain group of rather rigidly oriented young seminarians who had grown up in Christian homes, had gone to private Christian schools, a conservative Christian college, never had so much as the pimple or heard an expletive more shocking then "O, shucks". These young folks then came to a seminary to learn how to minister to a fallen, broken, bleeding world. Well I was just too much for them. So they decided I needed to be healed, exorcised, prayed over. It was very difficult for them to reconcile their theology with what they were encountering by knowing me. My friends had great respect for me as a Christian and for what they perceived as my ministry, certainly the areas of pastoring and teaching. And they were aware that my illness could prevent me from any further ministry and certainly from the mission field. So uninvited, they decided to intercede on my behalf. While their intentions were good, their rigid view of God's will and the way God works in and through people presented them from appreciating what was going on in this situation.

I have always found it to be very significant that Paul had what he referred to as his thorn in the flesh. Likewise Spurgeon suffered from clinical depression and Billy Graham was diagnosed with Parkinson's disease. And yet none of these men ever doubted God's ability to use them while they were sick but also through their sickness. The most difficult part of this whole problem for my young friends was that I personally felt no need of physical healing (and to this day never have). For me and in my experience, lupus has been a source of learning and a blessing. Not only has it tempered my vanity, but it has also protected me and my family from the natural consequences of the Type A personality by landing me in bed before I drove everybody else crazy.

Pain has helped me to find Christ at a deeper more personal level. Aloneness has forced me to be still in the company of the Holy Spirit. Chronic illness has helped me to identify with and empathize with the suffering of my clients. And yes I have been precluded from the mission field in the traditional sense. But that love of missions and especially for Africa has never died and in more than one instance God has allowed me to infect others with that love and they have gone to do what I've not been able to do. If all those who love mission work went into the mission field, who would be left home to pray in support?

To me the miracle is God working out his plan despite our interference; it is for us to be allowed to participate in and observe that plan being revealed. As I have aged and hopefully matured I have learned the importance of the big picture and found it sometimes less significant to focus on and quibble over details. It has always been so exciting for me to quietly go about my small task knowing that God is doing something very special. I always feel such a sense of expectancy. It's a little bit like Christmas morning, or perhaps my birthday, waiting for the gift to finally be on your lap. For many miracles are not something necessarily big and dramatic but they happen. They happen a lot and the trick is to see them.

I remember when I was a little child and I found or had been given a small injured wild bunny. I was given the care of the bunny and I built a cage with grass and bedding and water in it, and I even took the bunny to the veterinarian. While certainly all of this was helpful, the most important thing was that the bunny was really scared and as much as I wanted in my childish way to hold and comfort and soothe the bunny my parents told me that the more I forced my attention on the little guy the harder it would be on him. I spent long hours that summer sitting quietly right next to the cage, waiting and watching, and finally one day he came all the way over; and then he was sniffing at my hand, then slowly and carefully I picked him up and, after much sniffing and exploring, he nestled into the palm of my hand, and he wasn't shaking. That was a real lesson about patience and love, peace and celebration; a lesson I would repeatedly forget and relearn throughout the years. He and I became great friends that summer. That was a miracle.

When we must face chronic pain or illness, we are that bunny. We can experience the miracle of releasing the fear of our condition, freeing ourselves of thoughts of the unknown and resting our tired, hurting, confused selves in God's hands. Whatever happens will be "OK", knowing that God is with us in our trials. "*For thou art with me; thy rod and thy staff they comfort me.*" Psalm 23:4 (KJV)

God's comfort ushers in peace, and with peace can be joy – the joy derived from the security of being held by God. In turn, this provides freedom. Freedom from fear. Freedom from unrealistic expectations of achieving our own physical recovery. Freedom to share our experiences and empathize with others. Freedom to find humor in our condition.

Ed presents his story this way:

"For years I was in the position of caring for my wife, who was chronically ill. I couldn't fully understand the source of her strength, until I was diagnosed with a serious debilitating illness of my own. I tell people that God must have realized he wasn't being fair to us. He had showered my wife with all the spiritual blessings. Now he finally decided to even things up!"

Like the whale in *Whale's Lament* (the poem in the opening of this book), we may not have chosen our particular lot in life, but with God's help we may be able to *embrace our calling.*

5

COMFORTING ALONG THE WAY

comments by John Poorman

Demands upon the Comforter

The growth into wholeness in illness is never a solo journey. There are friends and family, loved ones and mere acquaintances who accompany us. Some may try to ignore our "differentness" out of an uncertain sense of how to relate. Others may be like Job's friends, counseling us toward healing, seeking causes for the unknown, leaving the burden of our illness in our laps.

Others, however, are able to embrace the notion of "comfort" in its Latin roots – that is, to be strong (fort) with (com). While not often given the gift of physical healing, each of us – if willing – can be Christ-present to those who are hurting, providing comfort, being "strong with", walking alongside the sufferer, offering strength for the weak.

God, of course, does not abandon anyone to true alone-ness, even if human comforters are not present. For God is the ultimate Comforter, walking beside us on whatever journey we may be facing.

What is called for in a human comforter? Simply to be "strong with" one in pain or illness is to reflect aspects of God's own comfort. Namely, to provide:

- acceptance of the sufferer in whatever condition she is in;
- independence when desired
- assistance when needed

- a "holding" environment which is safe and free of judgment
- forgiveness
- encouragement in enterprise, responsibility and ministry

These do not sound like terribly difficult comforts to provide, but our fallen nature and the fallenness of the world make them a challenge. Frustration attacks the would-be comforter when help is needed – once again – for what appears to be an easy task. Discouragement sets in when plans must be cancelled for the umpteenth time because of pain of sickness. Holding becomes demanding when it becomes viewed as a chore, getting in the way of other chores. And providing encouragement gets tiresome if it seems it is required continuously.

Consider Ellen's situation. She has a progressive neuromuscular condition:

"My daughter and son in law who live close by and help us a lot are on vacation in Florida. So, my husband is going stir crazy being locked in with me day after day. My care is more taxing now, as I can do less and less for myself. Now need help with eating, brushing teeth, wiping my face. I need his help constantly. He is beginning to be frustrated, impatient with me, and sometimes verbally and psychologically abusive. I cannot speak, especially if I start crying. Yet he demands explanations and seems to distance, walking away, saying, 'Well, I can't understand you until you quit crying, so I can't help you.' I feel as helpless as a newborn baby."

But the same God that informs the chronically ill individual that she is an intentional creation with purpose, gifts and ministries is also able to affirm the comforter that he is also an intentional creation and that his gifts and skills are intended for use (at least in part) in providing strength and stamina to the one who is lacking.

Scripture tells us that the Church (Christ's body at work in the world) is made up of many parts. We each are given a different role. Being a comforter, being the arms or legs or stamina for someone else does not *diminish* our value and take away from our own self-worth; rather, it *adds to it.*

In Bobby's case, she provided spiritual and emotional comfort (strength with) many individuals and couples over many years. Despite her physical challenges and limited strength, God used her as a source of inspiration and energy for many.

In our case (the nearly 34 years of time together on this earth), life was a partnership. We played different roles, roles which changed from time to time, but we always made an effort to find roles that were complementary. She wrote; I edited. She planned; I helped make those plans real. She found ways to continue to minister despite her obstacles; I committed myself to help make those ministries work. She preached; I sat in the congregation and frowned when I thought she chose her words poorly. (That last partnership wasn't the most constructive, as Bobby often pointed out to me.)

This was my vocation, but not my only vocation. Too often those placed in the position to be the "comforter" feel trapped, limited by the role. Like Ellen's husband. God does not intend this to be the case. Comforting is a calling and we must be willing to receive God's help and assistance from others in carrying out that calling successfully. But none of us – neither the individual with chronic illness nor the individual called to be the comforter – are single-dimension people. There must be outlets and opportunities for our *other* talents and interests, gifts and ministries.

For example, being a mother can be very demanding, but when it becomes all-consuming, things are likely to go awry. The marriage may suffer; the mother's health and emotional balance may suffer; the kids' sense of independence and self-worth may suffer. The mother must see the mothering role as but one, very important ministry – not her entire vocation. Similarly, the spouse or daughter, parent or sibling called to comfort one dealing with chronic pain or illness must see that calling as but one, very important ministry that must find its rightful place in the hierarchy of responsibilities and opportunities of life.

As demanding as life is upon the individual with chronic illness – that is, demanding in terms of letting go and allowing God to use the illness for ministry – life is equally demanding on the comforter. The comforter is called upon to be parent, confidant, physician and nurse as well as spouse (or child). Balancing those roles while staying healthy and emotionally balanced requires as much prayer and openness to God's miracles as that required of the individual with chronic illness.

In truth, all the requirements on the comforter that are listed above (providing acceptance, independence, assistance, holding, forgiveness and encouragement) are the requirements necessary for *all* healthy human relationships. But those in chronic pain and illness come closest of all of us to having needs that are similar to the dependent child described in Chapter 2. Like a child, the ill know they are not in a position to be fully independent. As Bobby noted about that condition, it is a gift from God to – as an adult – embrace the realization that we are dependent, in that it helps turn us toward God for strength and purpose.

Likewise, taking on the role of comforter (or having the role thrust upon us) can be seen as God's gift by providing a clear, concrete, valuable purpose in our life. How much closer to God can we get than being dependent upon Him for the wisdom and strength to be God's arms for carrying or God's hands for caressing our loved one?

In all of this, experience informs me that the greatest gift the comforter can provide along the journey is the holding. Figurative holding by providing a safe place. And literal holding – physical holding. A touch, an embrace, cannot be conveyed through mental telepathy. They must be provided physically, and are best provided often.

It is sad to say that, given our culture and the hard wiring of our brains, men are more likely to fail in the holding aspect of care-giving than any other. If I could do any part of the past 33 years over again, it would be to correct that aspect of my behavior – to be able to trade a few times of taking the trash out or running to the supermarket (acts of love in most men's minds) with a few more moments cuddling on the sofa, hand in hand.

Final Thoughts

Some pastors have received the high praise that "they never preach what they don't practice." For Bobby, it was said that "she never preached what she wasn't striving – through obstacles, occasional failures and successes – to practice." Finding wholeness within illness was a quest in which she succeeded beyond all human expectations. It was my privilege to have been a partner with her in her journey, an education in both how to live with illness and how to live with someone with illness, and a foreshadowing of our eventual life without pain or illness in the presence of God's glory.

About the Author

Roberta Suzanne (Andrews) Poorman was a beloved high school teacher, drama coach, Homiletics (preaching) instructor, ordained minister, pastor, preacher and Bible teacher, missionary, rape crisis and domestic violence crisis volunteer, pastoral counselor and administrator. Bobby also was an artisan in the media of photography, jewelry, natural soaps and candles.

She graduated with honors from Ithaca College and received both her M. Div. and D. Min. degrees with honors from Gordon-Conwell Theological Seminary. She married John Phillips Poorman – an urban transport planner, fine artist and occasional lay preacher – in 1980 and for over 33 years until her death in December 2013, Bobby and John were soul-mates and partners in life.

About this Book

Bobby's ministry was best realized through empathic, personal connection – particularly with the most vulnerable, broken individuals who came into her life as parishioners, clients, friends, family or strangers. Nearly twenty years ago Bobby was encouraged by friends and clients to share her scriptural understanding of wholeness and illness and its connection to ministry. She completed a partial draft at that time and shared it with advisors from Gordon-Conwell Theological Seminary. Bobby plunged into the next draft but was quickly sidetracked by dealing with her mother's Alzheimer's and cancer (her mother lived with Bobby and John for fourteen years) and her own renal failure. A kidney transplant, a move to Schoharie NY, God's call to leave pastoral counseling and serve the Schoharie Reformed Church and further renal failure put finishing the book on hold. Those who knew Bobby only in retirement will testify that her commitment to teaching and ministry never waned even after many more physical challenges were experienced in her later years.

Interest in her approach to ministry remains strong. The drafts were dusted off and completed for this posthumous publication.

www.ingramcontent.com/pod-product-compliance
Ingram Content Group UK Ltd.
Pitfield, Milton Keynes, MK11 3LW, UK
UKHW041925190726
13854UKWH00003B/1442

9 781304 787453